TEAM EARTH

SEED DISPERSERS
POOP, FUR, AND OTHER WAYS
ANIMALS SCATTER SEEDS

BY EMMA HUDDLESTON

CONTENT CONSULTANT
Amy Dunham, PhD
Associate Professor, Department of BioSciences
Rice University

Core Library

An Imprint of Abdo Publishing
abdobooks.com

Cover image: Birds commonly act as seed dispersers. They
swallow seeds and later poop them out elsewhere.

abdobooks.com

Published by Abdo Publishing, a division of ABDO, PO Box 398166, Minneapolis, Minnesota 55439. Copyright © 2020 by Abdo Consulting Group, Inc. International copyrights reserved in all countries. No part of this book may be reproduced in any form without written permission from the publisher. Core Library™ is a trademark and logo of Abdo Publishing.

Printed in the United States of America, North Mankato, Minnesota
102019
012020

Cover Photo: Roman Yanushevsky/Shutterstock Images
Interior Photos: Roman Yanushevsky/Shutterstock Images, 1; Andrea Izzotti/Shutterstock Images, 4–5; Shutterstock Images, 7, 10, 43; Maciej Matlak/Shutterstock Images, 9; Bonnie Taylor Barry/ Shutterstock Images, 12; Rich Carey/Shutterstock Images, 14–15; Scott Camazine/Science Source, 17; Paul S. Wolf/Shutterstock Images, 20, 45; The Art of Pics/Shutterstock Images, 23; Dr. Antoni Agelet/Science Source, 24–25; Suzanne Tucker/Shutterstock Images, 27; Duncan Usher/Alamy, 30; BBA Photography/Shutterstock Images, 32–33; Kelsey Green/Shutterstock Images, 34–35; Maks Narodenko/Shutterstock Images, 37 (left); Nataly Studio/Shutterstock Images, 37 (middle); Jerzy Gubernator/Science Source, 37 (right); Michael Potter/Shutterstock Images, 40

Editor: Marie Pearson
Series Designer: Megan Ellis

Library of Congress Control Number: 2019942034

Publisher's Cataloging-in-Publication Data

Names: Huddleston, Emma, author.
Title: Seed dispersers: poop, fur, and other ways animals scatter seeds / by Emma Huddleston
Other Title: poop, fur, and other ways animals scatter seeds
Description: Minneapolis, Minnesota : Abdo Publishing, 2020 | Series: Team earth | Includes online resources and index.
Identifiers: ISBN 9781532191015 (lib. bdg.) | ISBN 9781644943281 (pbk.) | ISBN 9781532176869 (ebook)
Subjects: LCSH: Seed dispersal by animals--Juvenile literature. | Seed dispersal by birds-- Juvenile literature. | Forests and forestry--Ecology--Juvenile literature. | Seeds-- Juvenile literature. | Plant propagation--Juvenile literature.
Classification: DDC 581.78--dc23

CONTENTS

CHAPTER ONE

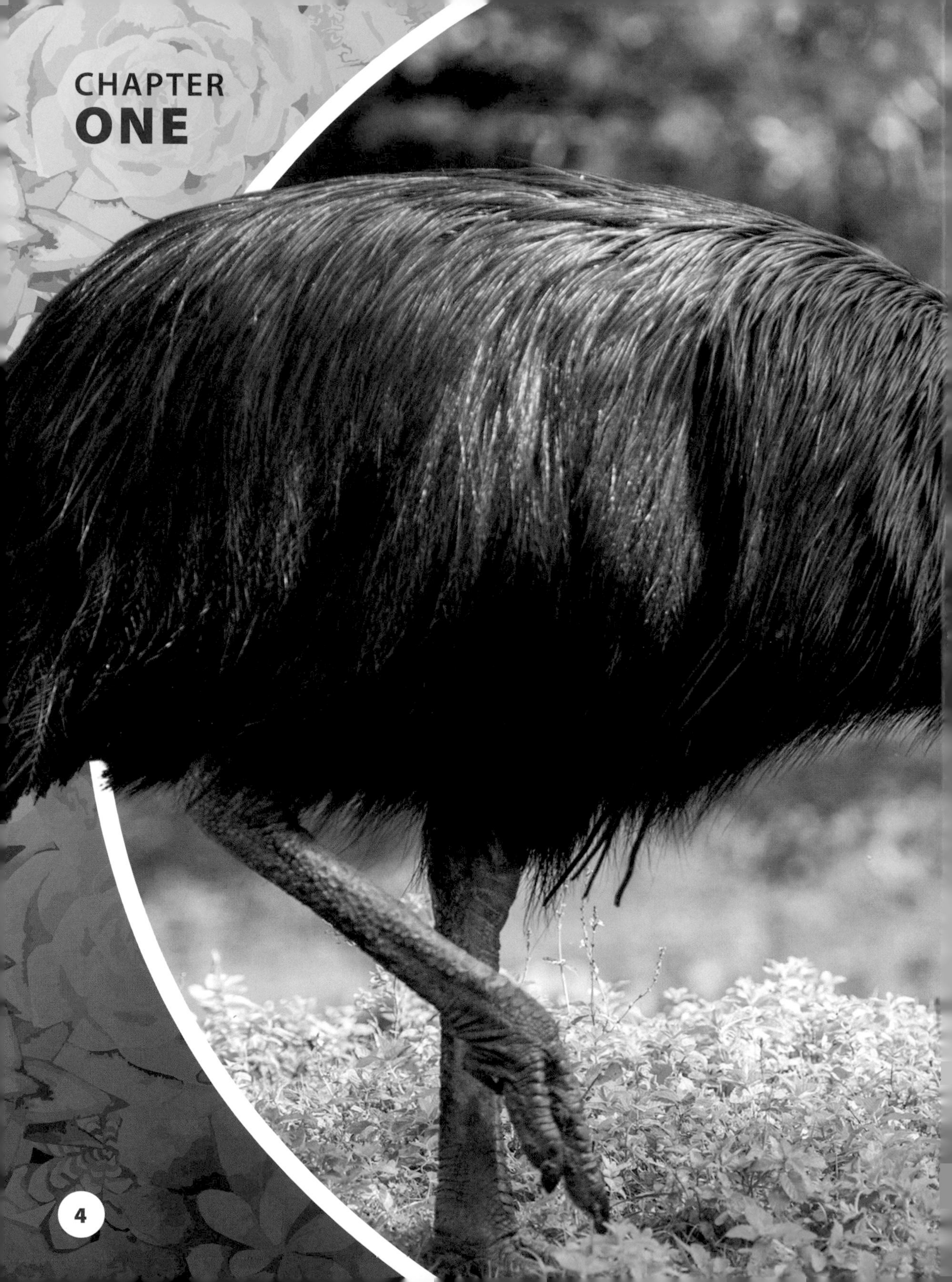

WHY SEEDS NEED TO SCATTER

A cassowary walks through a tropical rain forest. This large, flightless bird lives in northern Australia and New Guinea. It can stand up to 5.6 feet (1.7 m) tall. Bright blue, pink, and orange skin cover its head and neck. Thick, black feathers on its back protect it from thorny plants.

Cassowaries feed on large fruits. The cassowary is the only animal that eats certain fruits in the Australian rain forest. A rare type of rain forest tree, the *Ryparosa*, grows in Australia. It produces large orange fruits with

The cassowary helps disperse the seeds of many Australian rain forest fruits.

BLOWN BY THE WIND

Some plants use the wind to help them scatter seeds. Their seeds are lightweight. Sometimes the shape of the seed helps it fly in the wind. Maple seeds have a papery blade. It acts like a propeller and catches the breeze. Dandelion seeds have wispy strands attached to them that act like a parachute. Orchids are flowers that make the smallest seeds. The seeds trap air inside like a balloon. This makes it easy for the wind to blow them around.

a single seed inside. The tree relies on the cassowary as a seed disperser. A seed disperser carries seeds away from the plant that the seeds grew on.

When the *Ryparosa* fruit is ripe, it drops to the forest floor. The cassowary eats it by swallowing it whole. The bird's digestive system helps break up the outer layer of the seed so it can sprout later. Then, as the bird walks around, it scatters seeds when it poops. Very few *Ryparosa* seeds will sprout if a cassowary has not swallowed them.

PARTS OF A SEED

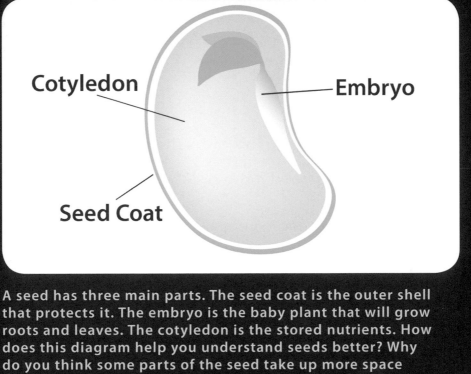

Cotyledon

Embryo

Seed Coat

A seed has three main parts. The seed coat is the outer shell that protects it. The embryo is the baby plant that will grow roots and leaves. The cotyledon is the stored nutrients. How does this diagram help you understand seeds better? Why do you think some parts of the seed take up more space than others?

BASIC PLANT SURVIVAL

A seed is an undeveloped plant inside a protective coat. Each plant species has a unique seed. Some seed coats are hard like shells. Others are thin or stretchy. Some seeds also store nutrients inside their coats. This helps them grow when the conditions are right.

More than 391,000 different plant species exist. The right growing conditions for each species are different. They include temperature, sunlight, water supply, and nutrients. For example, most grasses need four to five hours of sunlight a day. This gives them energy to grow. But some grasses need more or less than this.

The size of a seed can range from a speck of dust to larger than a dinner plate. The black specks in vanilla ice cream are the whole seeds of the vanilla orchid. The largest seed in the world comes from the coco-de-mer palm tree. It grows massive coconuts. They can be 19 inches (48 cm) long and weigh more than 40 pounds (18 kg). The palm tree's island habitat has rocky soil with few nutrients. So the tree stores lots of nutrients in its coconuts. That is why they are so large. This helps the seeds grow when they fall to the ground. The seeds are so large that they don't travel far. This helps keep them from ending up in the sea and dying.

The coco-de-mer palm tree grows in the Seychelles Islands in the Indian Ocean.

Seeds are often scattered after animals swallow and then pass them.

WHAT IS SEED DISPERSAL?

Parent plants are rooted in one place. This is why they rely on seed dispersers to scatter seeds. Seed dispersal keeps seeds from competing with the parent plant for food, water, or sunlight. With dispersal, seeds can grow in new areas and expand the species' habitat. Additionally, seed dispersal protects the species. If they are in multiple locations, they cannot be eaten or destroyed all at once. It also keeps them away from any predators feeding on the parent plant. These predators could kill a seedling.

Reptiles, birds, insects, and more scatter seeds. Some do it on purpose. They carry seeds or bury them in the ground. Others spread seeds by accident. This happens

EXPLODING PLANTS

Some plants have unique ways of scattering seeds on their own. The squirting cucumber fills with liquid as it grows. This builds pressure. When the fruit is ripe, it explodes if it is touched. The small cucumber falls off the stem. At the same time, liquid and seeds shoot out of the hole. The seeds can shoot 20 feet (6 m). Wild violets also scatter their own seeds. The seeds are tiny round balls. They are stored in a green case. As they grow, the case holding them dries out and shrinks. The pressure from squeezing makes the seeds pop out of the case.

Some birds eat berries, swallowing the seeds with the fruit.

when seeds get stuck to their fur or feathers. The most common way for animals to spread seeds is by eating them and pooping them out in a new location. Seed dispersers are essential for helping plants survive.

STRAIGHT TO THE
SOURCE

Thor Hanson wrote the book *The Triumph of Seeds*, about how seeds are important to human history. He also learned about scientist Charles Darwin, who lived in the 1800s. Darwin studied evolution. Hanson learned that Darwin was interested in seed dispersal:

Darwin was fascinated by how plants and animals were distributed around the world. . . .

In terms of the birds of the Galapagos, he recognized an association with South America, and began wondering how those plants were dispersed and how they could cross hundreds of miles from mainland South America.

Back in England, he began a series of experiments studying how seeds survive in saltwater and what happens when a seed lands in the soil.

Source: Simon Worrall. "How Little Seeds Shaped Human History in Big Ways." *National Geographic*. National Geographic, April 29, 2015. Web. Accessed July 3, 2019.

Back It Up

The author of this passage uses evidence to show that Darwin was interested in seed dispersal. Write a paragraph including two or three pieces of evidence the author uses to make this point.

CHAPTER
TWO

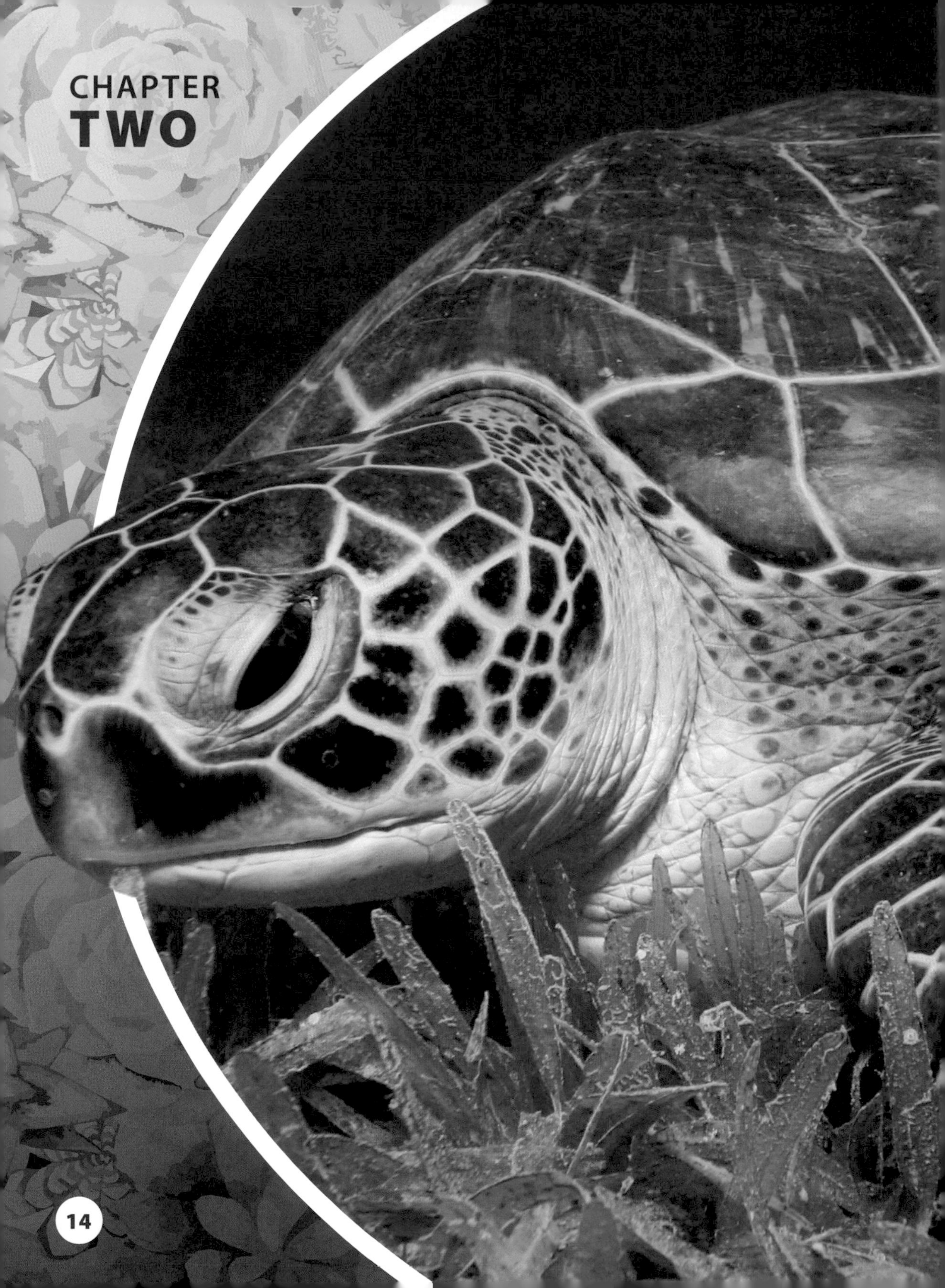

POOP

Many seeds are wrapped in fruit. The fruit attracts hungry visitors. Plants benefit from animals eating their fruit because the animals also swallow the seeds. The animals become seed dispersers by scattering seeds in their poop as they travel. This is the most common way seeds are dispersed.

Elephants disperse dozens of seeds. They eat up to 300 pounds (140 kg) of food each day, including fruits. They travel long distances and scatter seeds to different areas. Green sea turtles munch on sea grass. They spread several species around the ocean.

Seed dispersers aren't limited to land. Some, such as green sea turtles, spread seeds across the ocean.

ATTRACTING EATERS

Plants began growing fruit as an adaptation. Plants that grew tasty fruit survived better because animals would eat the fruit and scatter the seeds. Thousands of fruit species exist, and each one attracts specific seed dispersers. Bright colors such as red and orange stand out against the green and brown background of other plants. These fruits attract animals with good eyesight. For animals with poor vision, fruits attract them with a strong scent.

The jequirity bean plant does not grow fruit. But its seeds are bright red, mimicking fruit. Hungry birds see and eat the seeds.

Some violets and other plants rely on ants to spread their seeds. Myrtle wattles and long pink-bells attract ants to their seeds with elaiosomes. Elaiosomes are small, soft, fatty growths on the outside of a seed. They are full of nutrients for ants to eat. In fact, they mimic nutrients found in other ant food, such as insect

Wild ginger is one of the many plants that use elaiosomes to attract ants.

eggs. Without elaiosomes, the seeds would not benefit the ants. The ants would have no reason to collect or disperse them.

PROTECTING SEEDS

There are risks in using poop as a way to scatter seeds. Seeds can be destroyed by chewing. They can also be damaged in the digestive system. Many seeds are hard. This protects them from breaking down when chewed or digested. Some plants use color to protect delicate seeds from being eaten. Many plant buds are light green. This color is a sign that the fruit is not ripe yet.

It protects developing seeds because animals pass the plant by when looking for food.

Some plants use chemicals to protect their seeds. Bitter smells or tastes stop animals from swallowing seeds. They might spit seeds out after eating the flesh of the fruit. This happens with chili peppers. Capsaicin is part of chili pepper flesh. When a chili pepper is chewed, capsaicin irritates the skin inside the mouth. It causes the skin to feel hot. In the wild, this protects chili pepper seeds from rodents that would eat and destroy the seeds.

But birds are not affected by capsaicin. They disperse chili seeds. Birds swallow the chili pepper whole, so the seeds are still whole in their poop.

TRACKING TOUCANS

Seeds are an important food source for many birds. Most birds can eat up to half their bodyweight each day. A waxwing can eat 1,000 seeds in a day. Then they fly away and disperse seeds in their droppings. Tracking seed dispersal is very difficult. Still, scientists study it. They try to find out if or how plants are successful.

Toucans eat nutmegs whole. They digest the outer fruit layer. Then they regurgitate, or throw up, the inner seed. Scientists did a two-part experiment with toucans to study how they disperse nutmeg seeds. The first part included feeding toucans nutmegs to see how fast they ate, digested, and regurgitated the seeds. The second part of the study used GPS devices to see where and how far the toucans flew. Putting the two parts of the study together showed the potential

Toucans are native to Central and South American rain forests. They are important in keeping the forest diverse and healthy.

range of locations a seed from a nutmeg tree could be dispersed. The results showed that toucans regurgitated seeds approximately 25 minutes after being eaten. Most toucans dropped their seeds 472 feet (144 m) from the original tree.

SPECIAL SEED DISPERSERS

Some plant species wouldn't survive without the help of a specific seed disperser. The Galápagos tortoise disperses seeds for cacti and wild tomatoes on the Galápagos Islands. In Madagascar, many of the island's largest trees rely on lemurs to disperse their seeds. But most species of lemur are in danger of dying out because of forest clearing. This puts the trees at risk as well.

Pacu fish disperse seeds in Brazil's Pantanal. The Pantanal is the largest freshwater wetland in the world. It floods each year. During this

BIRDS IN HAWAIIAN FORESTS

Tropical forests on the islands of Hawaii need help recovering. Whole forests were cleared so grass could be planted for livestock to eat. In the mid-2010s, scientists looked for ways to grow native plants and trees in the forests again. They studied the role of birds in seed dispersal. For seven months in 2015, they collected seed rain samples. The collections included 3,717 seeds dispersed by birds from six plant species. This showed birds were very important for helping the forest recover.

flooding, many plants, such as the tucum palm, drop ripe fruit. Pacu swim through the water and eat the fruit. One fish that was caught had 141 seeds in its body. The fish disperse the seeds in their poop as they swim around. When the water goes down again, the seeds sprout in the soil.

Birds and other animals spread seeds in their poop. But this is not the only way animals help scatter seeds.

FURTHER EVIDENCE

Chapter Two talks about how animals disperse seeds in their poop. Identify the main point and some key supporting evidence. Then look at the website below. Find a quote that supports the chapter's main point. Does the quote relate to a piece of evidence already in the chapter? Or does it add a new piece of information?

SCIENCE LEARNING HUB: SEED DISPERSAL

abdocorelibrary.com/seed-dispersers

Lemurs swallow seeds when they eat fruit. There are some fruits that only lemurs disperse.

CHAPTER
THREE

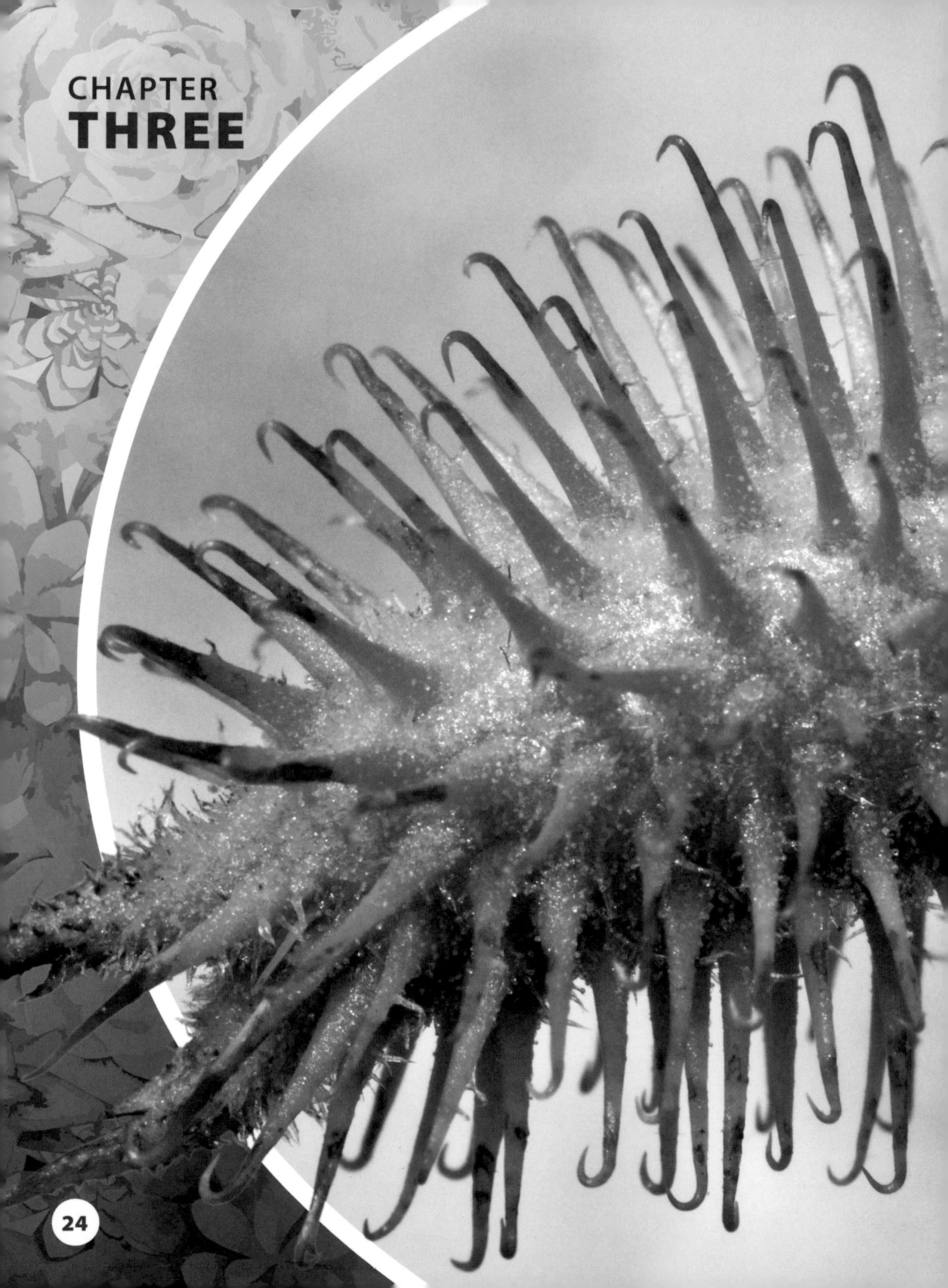

FUR AND FEATHERS

Many animals and birds transport seeds accidentally on their bodies. Some seeds have hook-like structures that latch onto fur. Others are covered in a sticky substance that attaches to feathers. Eventually the seeds are rubbed or scratched off. They can be dispersed at any time wherever the animal happens to be.

Plant species that rely on fur and feathers for dispersal do not use color or smells to attract seed dispersers. They try to hitch a ride without being noticed. This is because most animals try to remove things stuck

Some burrs have hooks on the ends to help them catch onto animals.

to their bodies. Scientists think this could be because carrying seeds on the body has no benefit for the seed disperser.

SEEDS INSPIRED VELCRO

George de Mestral was a Swiss engineer in the 1940s. One day he went hunting near mountains and riverbanks with his dog. Afterward de Mestral noticed small burrs stuck to his pants and his dog's fur. He wondered how they clung to his clothes. They even stayed on his dog after he rolled on the ground. De Mestral studied the burrs under a microscope. They came from the burdock plant. De Mestral got an idea. He invented a hook and loop fastener for clothing. Today it is known as Velcro. The interlocking design was based on the burdock plant's burrs.

BURRS

A burr is a prickly seedcase or flower. It helps seeds catch on fur, hair, or clothes. Burrs come in different shapes and sizes. Some have hooks, stiff spines, or other physical structures. Some spines cover the entire seed. Some hooks stick out of one end. Some prickly structures are a part of the flower. Agrimony has hooks on its sepals. Sepals are

Humans can act as seed dispersers when burrs catch onto their clothes.

the outer coverings of a flower bud. They are usually green. When the flower blooms, the sepals open up and become the undersides of the petals.

Burrs have multiple purposes. They protect the plant. Burrs look dangerous, and this keeps some animals from touching, eating, or harming the plant. Burrs also act as anchors for some species. Burdock plants are originally from Europe and Asia.

But humans have introduced them to most parts of the world. They have burrs with a hook shape. They often get caught in animals' fur. Many dog owners have returned from a walk to find they need to work these burrs out of their dogs' coats.

STICKY SUBSTANCES

Birds often disperse seeds with sticky substances coating the outside. These seeds attach to their feathers better than burrs. Birds hop along branches, search for insects, and fly through forests. During those activities, they come in contact with many plants.

The Pisonia tree grows on small islands in the Indian and Pacific Oceans. It relies on sea birds for long-distance seed dispersal. The tree's seeds are long and extremely sticky. They also have hooks. They can attach to birds and insects. However, the seeds can easily pile up. They can weigh down birds and prevent them from being able to fly. For this reason the Pisonia has been nicknamed the bird-catcher tree.

The sticky substance on seeds is useful for seed dispersal. But it often has another purpose. The coating protects the seed. It helps the seed stick when it lands in soil. This is important for the seed's survival. It can sprout when the right conditions are available.

In Southeast Asia, birds called flowerpeckers eat mistletoe. Mistletoe is a plant that grows on other plants. It has small berries. In order for a seed to sprout and grow, it must land on a tree branch.

HUMAN SEED DISPERSERS

Mammoths were the original seed dispersers for pumpkins. Mammoths died out long ago. Humans now plant pumpkin seeds, helping pumpkins survive. A study of grasslands in Sweden also found that humans help scatter seeds. People who work in nature can carry seeds on their clothes and shoes. In fact, another study showed that seeds on people's shoes can travel up to 6 miles (10 km). This can help spread seeds. However, it can also bring seeds to new places where they take root and become invasive. Invasive species can harm their new environment by competing for resources with native plants.

A mistletoe seed's stickiness helps it both cling to a bird until it is rubbed off onto a branch and stick to that branch so it doesn't fall out of the tree.

When flowerpeckers eat them and poop, the seeds do not fall to the ground. Instead, the seeds are sticky like glue. They stick to the bird's rear end. Sometimes flowerpeckers have to rub their bottoms on branches to remove the seeds. This spreads the seeds to new trees.

STRAIGHT TO THE
SOURCE

Soumya Prasad is a scientist who studies how human activity has affected seed dispersal. She talked about the effects in a 2012 interview:

> Climate change, fragmentation and animal declines are driving the seed dispersal process to the brink of extinction in most human-modified landscapes today.
>
> There are definitely ways in which an understanding of this process can improve the way in which we manage our landscapes. . . .
>
> The sooner we address the concerns surrounding seed dispersal in modern landscapes, the better we will be able to adapt to the changes in coming decades.

> Source: Mark Kinver. "Plants at Risk from Seed Dispersal Threats." *BBC News*. BBC, January 10, 2012. Web. Accessed July 3, 2019.

Consider Your Audience

Review this passage closely. Consider how you would adapt it for a different audience, such as your younger friends. Write a blog post conveying this same information for the new audience. How does your new approach differ from the original text, and why?

CHAPTER
FOUR

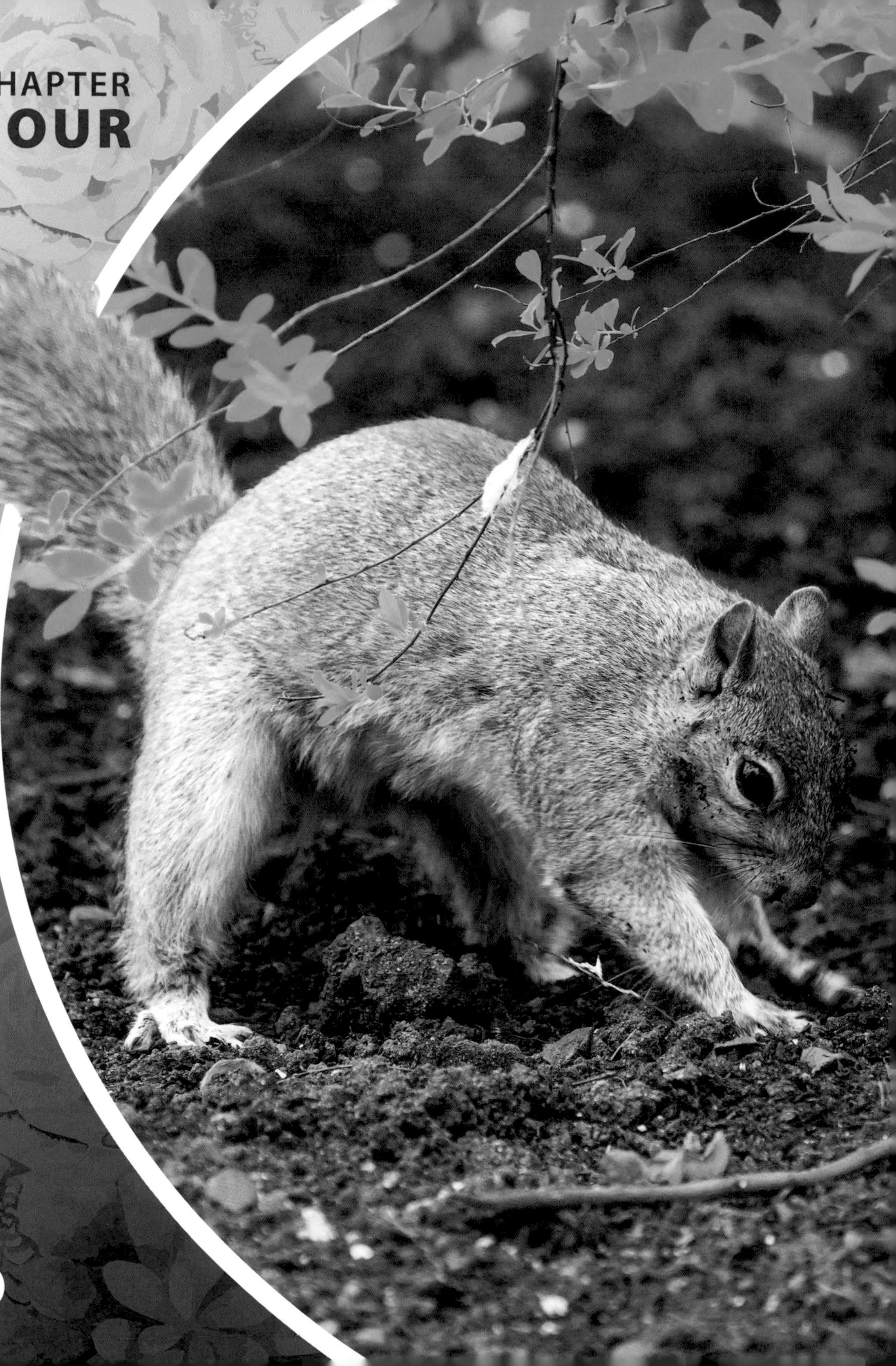

BURIAL

Seeds that are buried can have a higher chance of survival than those that land on top of the ground. When seeds are hidden underground, it is harder for seed-eating animals to find them. Additionally, being surrounded by soil can help the seed sprout. It allows the seed to easily get nutrients and water from the soil. At the same time, the seed is protected from the weather. Forest fires or too much sunlight can dry out seeds on the surface. If this happens, they cannot sprout.

Some animals bury seeds, including nuts, to store to eat later. Sometimes the animals forget where the nuts are. Other times the animals can't eat everything they stored. Then the seeds grow instead of being eaten.

Squirrels bury seeds to eat later.

The only plant that aardvarks eat is the aardvark cucumber.

Aardvarks normally eat termites and ants. The aardvark cucumber in South Africa is the only plant aardvarks eat. The plant's name comes from the fact that it depends on the aardvark to survive. It grows underground. The leaves of the plant can only be seen a few months of the year. This is unusual because most

plants show off their fruit. Otherwise animals won't see
it, eat it, or disperse the seeds. However, the aardvark
digs in the ground. It finds the cucumbers, eats them,
and scatters seeds in its poop. Then the aardvark buries
its poop. This helps the seeds sprout.

IS A NUT A SEED?

A nut is a dry, firm fruit. Its hard outer shell protects a single seed inside. Its shell is what makes it different from other seeds. Most seeds have a coating. It is not very hard and opens naturally when it is time to sprout. Nuts do not break open when they are ripe. They must be cracked open by a person or animal. Once the hard shell is opened, the seed has a chance to sprout and grow. Chestnuts, hazelnuts, and acorns are nuts. Despite their name, peanuts are not nuts. They are legumes. Legumes are fruits of plants in the pea family. Many have long, thin pods with multiple seeds inside.

Not all seeds are buried in soil. Some birds hide seeds in trees. The California woodpecker puts thousands of pecans, almonds, and acorns into holes in trees. Jay birds hide hazelnuts and acorns. The seeds sprout when they fall to the ground. Sometimes the birds drop them while flying. Other times the seeds fall into or around a tree. A study in Germany showed one jay could carry 4,600 acorns in a season. It dispersed the seeds 2.5 miles (4 km) from the original tree.

SEED DISPERSAL

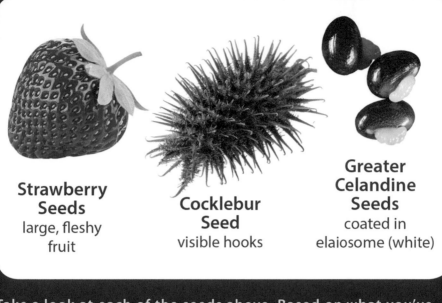

Strawberry Seeds
large, fleshy fruit

Cocklebur Seed
visible hooks

Greater Celandine Seeds
coated in elaiosome (white)

Take a look at each of the seeds above. Based on what you've learned about seed dispersal, which method of dispersal do you think each seed relies on, and why?

RODENT ACTIVITY

Rodents are small furry animals such as rats, mice, and squirrels. Many eat seeds. They destroy seeds by chewing them. In 2017 scientists in South Africa tracked the four-striped grass mouse and the hairy-footed gerbil. They took videos of the rodents' activity. They stuck bright yellow tags to the seeds to see where the seeds were stored. They could see the tags at night using a special light. One rodent species was active during the day, and the other was active at night. The study showed that the species that came out at night did more than eat seeds. It also helped disperse them.

Many rodents bury nuts. They are saving the nuts for when food sources are low. Sometimes they hide and move their pile multiple times. When rodents forget where they stored their nuts, the seeds have a chance to grow.

INSECT SEED DISPERSERS

Many insects, such as beetles, wasps, ants, and moths, eat seeds. These bugs may be small, but their actions help disperse seeds in several ways. They may bump into plants, knocking their seeds to the ground. Some small seeds get flown far distances on the insects' bodies. This often happens with bees. Their fuzzy bodies carry and disperse sticky seeds, such as those of the cadaghi eucalyptus plant.

A major way insects help plants survive is burying seeds. Ants are seed dispersers in Australia and dry regions around the world. Almost 5 percent of all flowering plants are dispersed by ants. The ants carry seeds into their colonies for food. They eat the elaiosomes on the seed. Fats in the elaiosomes give the ants energy. After the coating is gone, the ants don't need the seed anymore. They put it in underground tunnels without damaging it. The soil there is loose and fertile. The seed can easily sprout.

Dung beetles bury animal poop. Not only does this make the air smell better, but it helps plants. If the poop dried on top of the ground, it could block plant growth.

SEEDS THAT ATTRACT ANTS

Ants are attracted to chemicals in seeds. Seed coats with elaiosomes and sugars attract ants. Both adult ants and their larvae eat the elaiosomes. When ants finish with a seed, they store the seed underground. This helps the seeds, because it protects them from animals that might chew and destroy them.

Dung beetles roll poop into balls before burying it underground.

By rolling poop and burying it underground, the beetles return nutrients to the soil. They also bury any seeds in the poop.

Burial is important for many species to survive. In fact, some plants trick insects into burying their seeds. Dung beetles lay their eggs in poop because it helps their young grow. A grass species takes advantage of this behavior. Its seeds look like poop. This tricks dung beetles. They lay their eggs in the seeds, roll the seeds into a ball, and bury them. This disperses the seeds and successfully plants the grass.

MANY TYPES OF SEED DISPERSAL

Seed dispersal is a key part of plant survival. When seeds spread out, they can grow in new locations without competing for resources. All types of animals help scatter seeds. Many eat seeds and spread them in their poop. Sometimes they carry or bury seeds on purpose. Other times they accidentally spread seeds on their fur or feathers. Without seed dispersers, plant species around the world would struggle to survive.

EXPLORE ONLINE

Chapter Four talks about seed dispersers that bury seeds. Explore the website below. Compare and contrast the information there with information from this chapter about how plants benefit from seed dispersal that involves burial.

RODENTS HELPING TROPICAL TREES

abdocorelibrary.com/seed-dispersers

FAST FACTS

- A seed is made of an outer layer or coat, stored nutrients, and an undeveloped plant.

- Seed dispersers spread seeds from one location to another.

- Seed dispersal helps all members of a plant species survive. They do not have to compete with each other for resources if they are spread out. They can grow in new locations.

- Different kinds of insects, birds, bats, and other animals are seed dispersers. The main ways they spread seeds are in their poop, on their fur or feathers, and by burial.

- Many seed dispersers eat seeds and scatter them in their poop as they move. Sometimes digestion breaks down the outer layer of seeds and helps them sprout.

- The bright colors and strong scents of fruit attract birds and animals to plants. Some plants rely on one animal species to eat and scatter their seeds.

- Seeds with hooks, prickles, and burrs cling to fur. Seeds with a sticky substance on them attach to some birds. They later fall off or are rubbed off.

- Many seed dispersers accidentally spread seeds on their bodies.

- Some insects and animals bury seeds. This helps the seeds survive. They are hidden from creatures that might try to eat them. Additionally, the soil around them can help them sprout.

STOP AND THINK

Tell the Tale

Chapter Two of this book discusses the pacu fish as an important seed disperser. Imagine you are swimming with pacu fish in Brazil's Pantanal. Write 200 words about following a seed on its journey from the tree to becoming its own sprout.

Surprise Me

Many different types of insects, birds, bats, and animals are seed dispersers. After reading this book, what two or three facts about seed dispersers did you find most surprising? Write a few sentences about each fact. Why did you find each fact surprising?

Dig Deeper

After reading this book, what questions do you still have about how plants spread their seeds? With an adult's help, find a few reliable sources that can help you answer your questions. Write a paragraph about what you learned.

You Are There

Chapter One discusses what a seed is and why it needs to be dispersed. Imagine you are a scientist studying seed dispersal. Write a letter home telling your friends what you have learned. Be sure to include an example of a seed disperser and how it scatters seeds.

GLOSSARY

adaptation
a change that helps a living thing survive in a particular environment

colony
a group that lives together

fertile
containing nutrients to help plants grow

fragmentation
being broken or separated into parts

GPS
the global positioning system, which uses satellites in space to help figure out the location of objects on Earth

habitat
the place where a plant or animal lives

invasive
a living thing that comes from a different place on Earth and harms living things in its new habitat

regurgitate
to be spit out or thrown up

seed rain
a collection of seeds blown in the wind or fallen from birds

species
a specific type of plant or animal that shares traits and is able to breed with other members of that species

sprout
to grow or spring up from a seed

ONLINE
RESOURCES

To learn more about seed dispersers, visit our free resource websites below.

Visit **abdocorelibrary.com** or scan this QR code for free Common Core resources for teachers and students, including vetted activities, multimedia, and booklinks, for deeper subject comprehension.

Visit **abdobooklinks.com** or scan this QR code for free additional online weblinks for further learning. These links are routinely monitored and updated to provide the most current information available.

LEARN
MORE

Hirsch, Rebecca E. *Soil*. Minneapolis, MN: Abdo Publishing, 2015.

Huddleston, Emma. *Symbiotic Relationships*. Minneapolis, MN: Abdo Publishing, 2020.

INDEX

About the Author

Emma Huddleston lives in the Twin Cities with her husband. She enjoys writing educational books, but she likes reading novels even more. When she is not writing or reading, she likes to stay active by running and swing dancing.